THE HERITAGE COLLECTION

The Baobab Tree
Giant of the African Bush

Letitia deGraft Okyere

Illustrated by Masum Ahmed

Lion's Historian PRESS
Amplifying Authentic Voices

The Baobab Tree: Giant of the African Bush

Copyright © 2022 by Letitia deGraft Okyere

Illustrator: Masum Ahmed

Layout designer: Nasim Malik Sarkar

Library of Congress Control Number: 2022910311

All rights reserved.

No part of this publication may be reproduced, stored in a retrieval system, a database, and/or published in any form or by any means, electronic, mechanical, photocopying, recording or otherwise, without the prior written permission of the publisher.

ISBN 978-1-956776-07-2 hardback
ISBN 978-1-956776-08-9 ebook

Published by Lion's Historian Press
https://www.lionshistorian.net/

For

H.S.,

The Wind Beneath my Wings

Contents

Chapter 1: The African Baobab 1

Chapter 2: A Tree of Legends 3

Chapter 3: Ceremonies and Customs 5

Chapter 4: More Than One Thousand Years 7

Chapter 5: Bulky Tree Trunks 9

Chapter 6: Delicious Leaf Soups 11

Chapter 7: A Cucumber Shaped Fruit 13

Chapter 8: Reddish Black Seeds 15

Chapter 9: Large White Flowers 17

Chapter 10: The Tree Bark 19

Chapter 11: A Review of the African Baobab 21

Glossary 23

Quiz 25

References 26

Other Books in the Heritage Collection 27

Chapter 1

The African Baobab

The African baobab belongs to a small group of plants known as Adansonia, named after Frenchman Michel Adanson, who introduced the baobab to Europe around 1750. Mainland Africa has the Adansonia digitata, commonly found south of the Sahara Desert. There are six other types found on the east African island country of Madagascar and one in Australia.

Throughout history, the African baobab has been an important and sacred part of community life. They have a unique appearance — tall and thick — and are useful as a source of food, water, and shelter. African baobabs may grow to eighty feet tall, providing shade for people and animals.

In addition to acquiring local names like *Sagole* or *Kondanamwali*, the African baobab has nicknames. Some call it the *Upside-down Tree* because its bare branches look like tree roots. For others, it is the *Tree of Life* in recognition of its usefulness, or the *Monkey Bread Tree*, because its fruit, shaped like a cucumber, is beneficial to health, and also the *Bottle Tree*, because it stores water.

Chapter 2

A Tree of Legends

The African baobab has been the subject of legends. One story suggests that the baobab just appears, rather than grows from seeds like other plants. Other village elders tell stories of how baobabs walk at night and remain in one place during the day because their origins must remain a mystery. There is a popular story about the tree's unusual appearance, with different versions common to parts of Africa.

For example, the people who live along the Zambezi River in southern Africa teach their young that the baobab was once proud. It thought it was better than all the other trees in the forest because it was tall and majestic, though not exactly pretty looking. The forest keeper soon grew tired of the baobab's boasting and decided to teach it a lesson. One evening, after the sun went down, he uprooted the baobab and replanted it upside-down so it stopped being so proud. However, on the western coast of Africa, folklore tells that after the forest keeper planted the baobab tree, it just kept walking away. He got frustrated and uprooted the baobab and replanted it upside-down to keep it in one place.

Chapter 3

Ceremonies and Customs

The African baobab is central to cultural rites and protected by customs. *Wolof* speakers in West Africa make a dish of the fruit, seasoned with ground peanuts, nutmeg, and sugar, to be eaten after a child's baptism. During a war, when locals did not want enemies to discover the bodies of dead kings and chiefs, they buried leaders' remains in the hollow trunk of the baobab for protection.

Baobabs are a gathering place for locals to discuss political matters or simply to celebrate a happy occasion. They are also a place for special ceremonies. For example, as the dry season comes, natives gather under a baobab tree for rainmaking rites to encourage rain. In parts of Sudan, during initiation rights for young women into adulthood, community leaders provide baobab tree branches for fighting. A young girl becomes an adult when she proves her courage by defeating her opponent using a baobab tree branch.

Chapter 4

More Than One Thousand Years

The baobab is known to live to a great age. Scientists record that the Sagole, found in South Africa, is at least 1,200 years old. However, local Venda people argue the tree is close to 3,000 years old. Sagole is also known as the *Muri kungulwa*, or the *roaring tree*, because it makes a sound when the wind blows through its branches. The *Homasi* baobab, found in Namibia, lived at least 1,500 years, finally dying in 2004. The *Panke* baobab, in Zimbabwe, believed to have lived for 2,500 years, died in 2011.

A baobab's long life allows it to witness changes within a community across generations. If baobabs could speak, imagine the interesting history lessons they would give. Homasi, for example, could have told stories of Arab trade caravans from North Africa crossing the Sahara Desert to trade with merchants in the south. Then, decades later, Homasi witnessed the construction of roadways, making way for automobiles.

Chapter 5

Bulky Tree Trunks

The baobab is one of the biggest trees in the world. They can easily have a diameter of forty-six feet. It can take more than twenty men with outstretched arms to form a tight circle around its trunk. The living tree trunk can store water with its spongy and light wood. The *San* people of southern Africa used the baobab's stored water during seasons when there was no rain and rivers dried up. Also, because of their natural water content, baobabs cannot be destroyed by fire or lack of rain.

When the baobab's trunk becomes hollow because the wood inside dies, the tree produces new stems which, over time, fuse together. The people of Sudan, for example, use them as water tanks. Locals have turned hollow trunks into homes, capable of holding thirty people at a time. Other communities converted hollow trunks into shops, chapels, and prisons. The *Ombalantu* baobab in Namibia has had such purposes, including a post office and hideout during conflicts.

In Zambia's Kafue National Park, tourists enjoy visits to the *Kondanamwali* baobab or *the tree that eats maidens*. Local lore tells how Kondanamwali fell in love with four young women from the village. The women rejected Kondanamwali's love and married men from local communities. Kondanamwali grew hurt and angry, seeking revenge. During a storm one night, he opened and pulled in these four maidens and kept them imprisoned within his walls. Thus, on stormy nights, villagers believe they hear the four maidens crying for help.

Chapter 6

Delicious Leaf Soups

For people south of the Sahara Desert, the African baobab's leaves are a regular part of their meals. Some groups use the baobab leaf like spinach and put it in soups, stews, and other sauces. It can be eaten with vegetables like cassava or yam, or grains like millet. The leaves are as healthy as carrots or cabbage and help thicken soups and stews. In some cultures, a favorite dish is baobab leaf stew mixed with cowpea and sweet potato cooked in peanut oil. For poorer populations, the leaves are a good replacement for expensive beef and chicken.

As a result of its good nutritional value, sick people eat baobab leaf soup for strength. In Ghana, mothers give leaf soup to babies to move them from milk to solid foods. Animals like camels and donkeys reach for leaves for feeding or pick on those that have fallen to the ground. In Nigeria, farmers pound baobab leaves for horses to improve their strength.

Chapter 7

A Cucumber Shaped Fruit

The baobab produces a fruit that can grow as large as melons. It has a hard case, which, when opened, shows its dry and mushy pulp. The locals know that the fruit, with its sweet, tart taste, has many health benefits, rich in vitamin C. The hard case is waterproof and made into calabashes or small shells for castanets.

A common use of the fruit is a cooling drink. However, across Africa, diverse cultures have ways of eating fruit pulp. Some may eat it with milk in porridge made from maize, millet, or rice, and others may enjoy the fruit like a mango. Mothers may dry the pulp and grind it into flour used to flavor breakfast dishes or used as a raising agent like baking soda. Other times, mothers soak the pulp and mash it into a drink or ice cream. In European shops, packaged powdered African baobab pulp is available for mixes with water or milk for healthy beverages.

CHAPTER 8

Reddish Black Seeds

The fruit contains reddish black seeds, which are also nutritious. They have kernels that are difficult to separate from the outer seed cover. As a result, locals commonly eat the whole seed. The kernels taste like almonds, and the French use them in making a type of almond cake. The seeds can be pressed for oil which is used on the skin.

Locals eat baobab seeds raw or soaked and roasted for easy digestion. Others may boil and dry before eating. Mothers ferment and grind seeds which they add to maize, millet, or other porridge. Mothers also add water to fermented seeds, which they pound and make into balls for soups.

Chapter 9

Large White Flowers

The African baobab's flowers are large and white. The white flowers take a long time to show on plants, up to twenty years. They open at night and last for only a day. They have a strong, unpleasant smell making it difficult for humans to enjoy their edible nature. However, in certain parts of Africa, locals eat baobab flowers as a snack or use them for making drinks.

The white flowers, however, are more useful in animal life. As flowers bloom at night, it is suited for the bats, attracted by its strong, reeking smell. Bats feed on the flowers' nectar and are useful in the plant reproduction process, known as pollination. Other larger wild animals also feed on the baobab's flowers.

Chapter 10

The Tree Bark

The tree bark is useful to local communities. It is soft, fibrous, and fire-resistant. Craftsmen use the fiber to produce rope, thread, and strings for local musical instruments. Weavers also produce fabric used for making bags. In Senegal, locals weave the fiber into rain hats and vats for carrying water.

The bark is also used for medicinal purposes. Mothers and grandmothers soak tree bark in water for days and bathe their sons and grandsons with the baobab water. They believe it helps boys to grow strong and tall. In northern Ghana, mothers give the bark's gum-like substance to babies to help with weight gain. Locals use the bark's substance to make soap, rubber, and glue. Wild animals like giraffes and elephants chew on the tree bark to extract its sap.

Chapter 11

A Review of the African Baobab

The African baobab — digitata — was the first to be discovered. It has inspired songs and poems, received the protection of local communities, and supported both human beings and animals with daily living. There is no end to the uses of the African baobab. Even its roots have functions. Older roots, though not edible, provide a rich red dye, and young roots are edible and used in stews and soups.

Writings from as early as the 11th century mentioned the tree, when local doctors used its fruit to cure fevers. Across Africa, its significance is undeniable. In Niger, for example, priests inscribed religious scripts on baobabs. In Sudan, these trees marked battlegrounds. Government leaders in Senegal selected the baobab as the national tree. In South Africa, the Order of the Baobab is a national honor for excellent service in business, science, technology, and community development. In Mali, African baobabs mark points on maps. Even travelers to West Africa sought to be associated with its majestic giants. European explorers, such as Henry the Navigator, marked their names on baobabs. Its legendary status led to its leading role in animated movies such as the Tree of Life in Disney's *Lion King*.

Glossary

Madagascar — Madagascar is an island country off the east African coast in the Indian Ocean. Its official languages are Malagasy and French.

Zambezi River — The Zambezi or Zambesi flows from Zambia into the Indian Ocean. Its name means Great River, and it travels over the famous *Mosi-oa-Tunya* (Victoria) Falls.

Namibia — Namibia, or officially the Republic of Namibia, is in southern Africa, sharing a border with the Atlantic Ocean. Its largest and capital city is Windhoek.

Kafue National Park — The Kafue National Park, located in Zambia, is one of the largest parks in Africa. The Kafue is home to diverse wildlife.

Calabash — A hollow fruit shell used as a container.

Cassava — Cassava is a starchy vegetable that grows in the ground. The cassava root, covered in a rind that is easily removed, is long and tapers at the end.

Yam   Yam is a vegetable from a plant that forms tubers. Yam has a tough brown skin that is removed before cooking.

Kernel   The kernel of a nut or fruit is usually the inner soft and edible part. For example, if you removed the shell of a nut, you would find the kernel within.

Pollination This is the process whereby pollen from the male plant is transferred to the female plant for reproduction.

Castanets   Small shell-like pieces that are strung together to make a musical instrument used by dancers.

Quiz

1. **Who introduced the African baobab to Europe?**
   - (a) Henry the Navigator
   - (b) Michel Adanson
   - (c) Forest keepers
   - (d) Clement Adanson

2. **Why is the African baobab nicknamed the Upside-down tree?**
   - (a) It is tall and ugly looking
   - (b) It stores water
   - (c) It is a very useful tree
   - (d) Its bare branches look like tree roots

3. **Which African baobab is believed to swallowed up four maidens?**
   - (a) Sagole
   - (b) Homasi
   - (c) Ombalantu
   - (d) Kondanamwali

4. **What color is the flower of the African baobab?**
   - (a) Green
   - (b) White
   - (c) Yellow
   - (d) Pink

Quiz Answers: BDDB

References

Bamalli, Zahrau, et al., "Baobab tree (Adansonia digitata L) parts: nutrition, applications in food and uses in ethno-medicine - a review." (2014).

Wickens, G.E., and Lowe, Pat. *The baobabs: Pachycauls of Africa, Madagascar, and Australia.* Germany, Springer Netherlands, 2008.

Wickens, G.E., The baobab: Africa's upside-down tree. *Kew Bulletin,* vol. 37, no. 2, 1982, pp. 173-209.

Nour, A.A., et al., Chemical composition of baobab fruit (Adansonia digitata L.). *Tropical Science,* vol. 22, no. 4, 1980, pp. 383-388.

Maheshwari, J. K., "The Baobab Tree: Disjunctive distribution and conservation." *Biological Conservation* 4 (1971): 57-60.

Other Books in the Heritage Collection

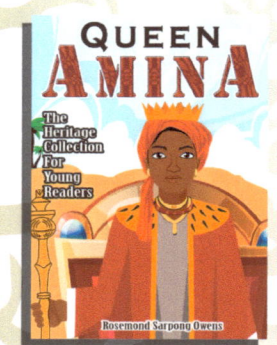
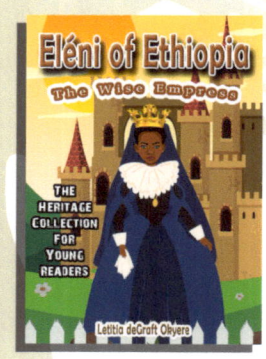
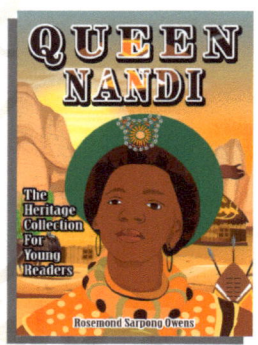
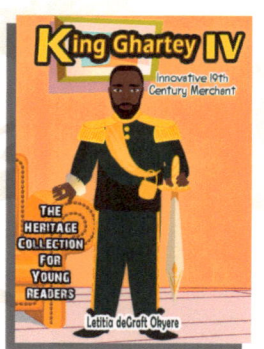
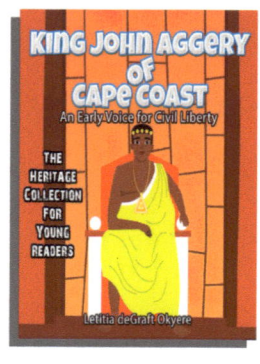

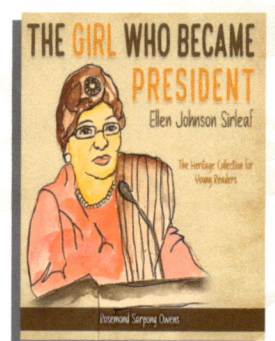

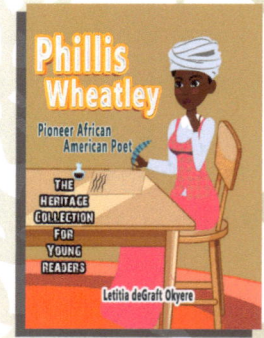
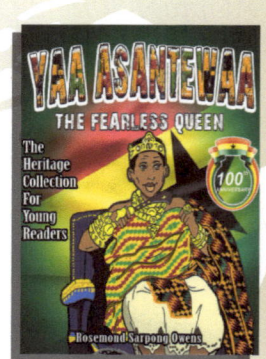